REFLECTIONS ON FAMILIES

JACQUE LEONARD

Published 2025

Printed in the United States of America

First Edition

ISBN (softcover): 978-1-967842-92-6
ISBN (e-book): 978-1-967842-93-3

For information, address:

Holzer Books LLC
8 The Green, Ste. A
Dover, Delaware 19901 USA

For information about special discounts available for bulk purchases, sales promotions, and educational needs, contact:

info@holzerbooksllc.com
+1 (888) 901-7776

holzerbooksLLC©

CONTENTS

Poems to Give You Strength

PART I

Poems for a Mother's Heart

TURN ON YOUR LIGHT

As women of faith we have a great chance
To help and find others, their lives to enhance.
Be part of the growth of these last day's work.
Let's turn on our lights and from others not shirk.

We reach out to others, relationships grow.
We seek faithful women who godly ways know.
Yes, those who seek righteousness, selfish thoughts shun,
We see their integrity like the Son.

Be part of this work in the upcoming years.
Be righteous and stand out from most of your peers.
Be different in ways that bring honor to Him.
Be known as articulate, light bright, not dim.

Let's learn how to brighten the light that we have;
Be distinct as we follow the Gospel's straight path.
Wear a smile as you go through your life day by day.
Shine your light and show others that you know the way.

TEACHERS OF MEN

The daughters of Eve have been given a gift
'Tis the gift and the power to touch lives.
Within each of us is a tender soft heart
And a drive to reach out and to lift.

We look on the folks all around and see need,
Then we reach out to change through our love.
In time we all learn that we can't make them change,
But in love we just softly plant seeds.

It's love in our hearts for the one and the all
That brings out our great need to reach out.
To teach and to touch and to help is the drive
That enables those touched to stand all.

LITTLE ONE
WITH THE SPARKLING EYES

Oh, my little on with the sparkling eyes and the indomitable spirit,
I know this home is not a fit place for thee. Trust me, I will make it better.
I will care for thee.

Is not this orphanage better, my little one? Trust me, it will soon be better still.
Thou art in my hands, little one with the sparkling eyes.
I will care for thee.

You see, little one? This home is better.
Here you can heal two broken hearts; and in the process, your own will heal as well.
Thou art in my hands, little one with the sparkling eyes.
I care for thee.

I know it hurts that this kind father is gone, little one, but he is in my hands.
It is right for you to be here, you have a work to do.
Thou art in my hands, little one with the sparkling eyes.
I care for thee.

Thou art doing well, little one with the sparkling eyes.
I know this new land to be a good one. Trust me, little one of the sparkling eyes.
This land will be good to thee.
I care for thee.

Oh, how I know it hurts to lose one who has taught you so much and helped you to grow,
but I will help you make a legacy to her. She is in my hands now.
You, too, are in my hands, little one with the sparkling eyes.
I care for thee.

Here you are at a new stage and place in your life. I have led you here.
You have little ones of your own to care for. I will help thee.
Thou art, as always, in my hands, little one with the sparkling eyes.
I ever care for thee.

This poem was created as a part of an interview job I had while helping build a website. This story, as told to me, is this man's story of his life, which though hard, was always guided and blessed. It touched my mother's heart.

VIRTUE

How can I know if I am virtuous enough?
How can I know what it means?
What is the source of the depth of this word?
Why does it hold such allure?

Through centuries of time it has served as a goal
Of all who would live high ideals.
Within our own minds we all have a clue
Of just what we think that it means.

Great tomes have been penned that list virtues galore
And tell of their presence or lack.
Yet, it need not be daunting to get at the root
And know all that virtue demands

Virtue is living a life that is pure,
Pure in intent and life lived.
It means that the best that is known by a soul
Is practiced day in and day out.

The depth of this word hints at values divine
Shared by those who are bearers of truth.
When practiced in lives, there's incredible peace;
Seek out virtue and live what you learn.

On the Loss
of a Beloved Mother

There's an ache in your heart
That shows you're a part
Of a special affair of the soul.

For a time you may cry
'Til the tears have run dry,
Then you'll go forth to honor her truths.

As her daughter you know,
Though the time may go slow,
What she wants you to do with your life.

When her soul left this life,
She returned as a wife
To the one she had left years ago.

She has gone on ahead
On the path that you'll tread,
When your time on this planet is done.

Let the memories be sweet,
'Til in Heaven you meet.
Live so honor will sweeten that day.

A MOTHER AND HER SON

All over the world there are mothers with sons
And most often the bond grows quite strong.
But once in a while a special bond runs,
That makes heaven burst out into song.

This bond is so deep and so strong that it holds.
Doesn't matter, rebellion or hurt.
This mother forgives and forgives and ne'er folds,
For she loves him no matter the hurt.

In a time when rebellion has lessened its grip
And results leave son less than before,
This mother loves on and shows care through life's trip,
And her love grows to something much more.

The bond then is firm and the love full and wise.
Doesn't matter the distance or pain.
This mother assures that his spirit will rise.
It's a bond no one needs to explain.

DAUGHTER OF HEAVENLY FATHER

I am a daughter of Heavenly Father,
Sent here to learn and to grow.
I have been given a yearning to know
And much help as I search out their will.

I have a brother who patterned the way,
Gave me the keys to get home
Left me directions in case I did roam
And paid for my sins with His life.

When I am quiet and search for the way,
Help comes through scripture and song.
When I am open, there's help when I'm wrong,
And I know I am guided and led.

When I have finished the work of this life
When I have learned what I must
Then I'll return, for in this I can trust
Heavenly Parents will welcome me home.

DAUGHTER OF GOD

Who am I to boldly proclaim that I am a daughter of God?
You may ask, "Isn't that being rather presumptuous?"
On what do I base this bold declaration?
Check out this reasoning.

If He is my Heavenly Father, then I am His earthly daughter.
If He is God, then I am a daughter of God.
If I am a daughter of God, then it stands to reason that I may have inherited some of His characteristics.
I may also stand to inherit some things of tangible value.

How do I even know that I have a Heavenly Father and/or that He exists?
I'm a thinker. I watch, study, read, ponder and process what I have found.
Here's what I know.
I know that this body that I inhabit is wonderfully and miraculously made.
I know that it contains fail safes and backup systems unlike anything mankind has ever been able to duplicate.

Within this universe that we inhabit, there are systems within systems within systems and
I am just a little part of this whole.
Yet for all of my insignificance in the grand scheme of things, I know that I am precious
to Him.
I have received comfort in dark times that has no rational explanation.

This comfort is part of my inheritance as His daughter.
I have also inherited, from Him, a heart that cares.
I have a mind that can reason.
I have a link to His other children.
I can look at my brothers and sisters and see bits of Him in them.
He is linked to me through my thoughts.
He sends me thoughts and ideas to help in times of need, mine and others.
He has given me music, books, prayers and companionship.
I can feel it and that cannot be denied.

YOU ARE WHAT I WANT YOU TO BE

Lyrics by: Jacque Leonard

Music by: Carrie E. Rounsefell
Arranged by: Jacque Leonard

2. Just live each day with love in your heart,
Spreading cheer to all you see.
There are burdens to lift, with each word that you say,
Souls longing to be set free.
Look to me my child, to be thy guide,
Though dark and rugged the way.
Be strong, have courage along the path,
To say what I want you to say

Just go where I want you to go, Dear Child,
Ever nurturing body and soul.
Just say what I want you to say,
Dear Child, just be what I want you to be.

3. I know, Dear Child, of the work you've done
The hearts that you have caressed.
Just know for this work that I'm greatly pleased;
Just know that you will be blessed.
So trust thy all to my tender care,
Please know that I do love thee.
You've done my will with a heart sincere;
You are what I want you to be.

You've gone where I told you to go, Dear Child,
Ever nurturing body and soul.
You've said what I told you to say, Dear Child;
You are what I want you to be.

Your Hurts, His Arms

When life's trials burst upon you,
And you feel to fail to try,
It may be a time to have a cry,
And lean upon His stronger arms.

Grab a handkerchief right then
And then give yourself some space.
Don't worry 'bout your tear stained face,
Just lean upon His stronger arms.

Time will pass and your wounds'll mend,
With new strength, you'll carry on.
That strength flows in and hurt is gone.
You leaned upon His stronger arms.

Guardians of the Hearth

Oh it's easy to see how a mother might be
The best guardian of the hearth,
If we look we can see that this title might be
For women whatever their role.

As a sister to some we can shoulder a load;
We look to their safety and care.
As an aunt we can know if there's need for some aid,
Provided we just keep in touch.

E'en a grandma can know, when her heart is attached,
If help would be welcome indeed.
Be it cousin or niece, or granddaughter or wife,
There's need that requires all our love.

All women were made with a heart built to love,
And people all 'round need our strength.
We are tied to each other by threads of all types;
Just feel the pull and respond.

OUR SPHERE OF INFLUENCE

Women of the world, no matter where they live,
Have within their nature, the aching need to give.
Such nature serves a purpose throughout the weary world
No matter what our station, compassion's seldom furled.

Thus we touch the hurting within our local sphere
Soften harsh conditions, and spread a word of cheer.
Our influence may impart a more righteous path to take,
And lead a wavering soul to a path from bad mistake.

When we stand for righteousness, evil loses power
Good we say and good we do causes evil to cower.
So, gather up your righteousness, no matter where you live;
And know that you can change your world, knowing what to give.

Mothers Who Know

Years ago in this land there existed a troop
An unusual group of brave sons.
They were taught by their mothers to follow God's law
And to walk towards His light every day.
They were told by their mothers that if they had faith
Their God would protect them from harm.
They all fought together to aid a great cause
And not one lost their life in the fight.

All our children today may not gather to fight
In great troops of two thousand at once,
But the enemy's out there just laying in wait
For the weak who were not taught at home.
For the mothers who know are aware of the risk
And they know how to succor their own.
They've made their promises to Him and can influence their heirs;
They have power for good in their lives.

And those mothers who know have desires that run deep
To bear children and nurture their faith,
To provide them with models of righteous desires
And to guide them towards heavenly goals.
They gain knowledge and wisdom then teach to inspire
And good order is everywhere seen.
There's a goal and a focus on leading at home
Though the world calls others away.

There have always been mothers who know and have faith
Those who nurture the paths of their heirs.
With the enemy of righteousness outside the doors
There's a need for an army prepared.
It's the mothers who know that will send those with power
To the battle that wages without,
And those youth in the thousands will fight 'gainst the foe
And nary a one will be lost

THE NURTURING DRIVE

There are little ones coming to live in our world,
Precious ones, dear to His heart.
He cannot be here to see to their needs.
Who can He find to extend them His love?

Who will see that they have what they need every day?
Teach them to live and to love?
Find them when one wanders far from the way,
Who will then find them and bring them back home?

Just such questions were asked ere He sent the first one.
Answers were found for each need.
Planted within every woman He made,
Deep need to nurture young life so to thrive.

'Twas His plan that a woman has need to reach out.
Teach and protect and inspire
Many are needed to answer this drive.
Broad is the way thus to serve previous souls.

As a daughter of God, look around; see the need.
Answer the deep-seated call.
Nurture the previous of God as you're lead.
Feel His approving regard; fill your soul.

PART II

Poems for Moms and Dads

THOUGHTS ON MARRIAGE

First comes love, and then comes marriage;
Then comes babe in baby carriage.
We've grown with this in back of mind.
Perhaps to truth we've become blind.

Sometimes truths that once seemed ageless,
Start to change in minds and pages.
Before we change our values dear,
It's good to look at things most clear.

Heavenly Father's plan laid plainly,
Taught us how to live most saintly.
He wants each child with Mom and Dad,
With both involved and all quite glad.

Marriage is His plan for families;
Love, and train and live quite grandly.
This goal is grand and quite ideal;
It's clear to see its broad appeal.

First ask Him just how He wants us.
Seek out help to live His justice.
He'll help you find your balance dear.
Your family plan couldn't be more clear.

IN HIS IMAGE

Lyrics by: Jacque Leonard

Music by: Jacque Leonard
Arranged by: Jacque Leonard

2. Now we know how He looks and we know He does care
Like a father He loves, wants what's best.
Gave us Holy Ghosts Fire, gave us rules, sent His heir;
Sent us down to this world as our test.
Chorus

3. Will we follow His plan for Salvation for all?
Will we love all His children on Earth?
Will we practice obedience and answer His call?
Will we show Him we know of our worth?
Chorus

WATCHCARE

The most basic needs after food, water, clothes,
Is the need to feel safe, to belong
So we join into groups to provide this goal
Then we guard and protect all within.

There's a system of **care** that Our Father requires.
It's for all who would strive Him to please.
We provide for the **watchcare** of all we're assigned,
Looking o'er them throughout all our days.

It might mean we provide them a meal or two;
It might mean that we help with their chores.
But however it plays on throughout all our days,
There is someone who **watch**es and **care**s.

All our job is to do as our Father requests,
And look out for the people around,
Just to **watch** them and notice when e're there's a need
And to meet it with all of our **care**.

ODE TO THE
CHRIST-CENTERED HOME

There is a home, a Christ-Centered home, wherein the blessed dwell.
In that home, the Christ-Centered home, pure love doeth anger quell.
All feelings, tender feeling, all are nurtured in this home
From such a home, a Christ-Centered home, there's no desire to roam.

How is it made, this Christ-Centered home from which none wants to leave?
To make a home just as this, each member must believe.
Believe in tending all the thoughts, the deeds, the words and hearts.
Believe in study, prayer and song as each one does their parts.

In such a home, the Christ-Centered home, the Natural man relents.
If anger comes the members there know quickly to repent.
The home is neat and clean and calm with pictures that inspire
When music plays it often seems like from a heavenly choir.

There's often talk in such a home on how each can reach out.
When guests come in they're treated well and seldom hear a shout.
They oft join in the family fun as gentle laughter sounds.
At end they gather everyone as prayer is heard around.

In such a home, work is enshrined; it's what is taught and done.
Mistakes are made, but lessons learned, and harm occurs to none.
No matter what the challenges, each member knows their worth.
Oh may our homes be just such homes more often on this earth.

Gaining

needed

strength

PROTECTING FAMILIES

Ever since families have been on this earth,
There has been a desire to protect.
There are things in this world that will bring them great harm
So to guard them is always correct.

How can we do it; how can we be safe?
Is there some way that families can find?
There are answers for all with a will to reach out,
For our Father wants none left behind.

Answers are found in the Heavenly Plan
That's designed to bring peace to us all
For it helps us make families eternally sealed,
And it gives us new strength when we fall.

Time with our families spent every week,
Set aside with intent for us to teach,
Brings us closer to Him as the scriptures we search,
And a Heavenly protection we reach.

Work is required to have what we want,
Nothing worth it comes easy and quick.
So, establish your house with much order and prayer
And protection you'll build brick by brick.

Strengthening Families and Homes

Strong families are families where love abounds,
Where virtue is taught and the Lord is crowned.
Strong families form homes that are full of peace,
And repentance is present with practiced ease.

To reach this nirvana takes constant care.
See music and scriptures and order there.
It's daily an effort to share life's load,
And all selfish passions must hit the road.

Each day there is prayer offered many times
Alone and in concert to clear out grime.
Strong families are pure, ever printed to serve,
With homes that are havens, yet full of verve.

Where learning is crowned as the boon it is;
Without it our strength soon becomes a hiss.
Where books, and discussions and truths abound,
'Tis there that the family is safe and sound.

PARENTHOOD

There's a plan built for happiness geared for us all,
And there's many who've found it with joy.
The grand plan calls for families to answer the call,
And bring children to homes to enjoy.

It's a truth that with children, come worry and work,
Yet there's lightness and laughter and love.
And sometimes it's so hard we are tempted to shirk,
Yet we know they are gifts from above.

There's quite a few people who want to partake,
And they've tried every trick in the book.
Yet the failure of year after year their faith shakes,
And they wonder, were they overlooked?

There is more than one way to be part of this plan,
E'en if timing or chance says not now.
There are neighbors, and friends who would be your best fan
If you just offered time with a vow.

Almost all can be parents in some little way
As we open ourselves to the call.
At all stages of life, we've a need to obey.
Share the love that you have, share with all.

Grandparents

A valuable part
of nurturing
the family

Nurturing the Rising Generation

A child is like a precious plant.
Its needs are much the same.
Each responds to love and care,
Some water now, choice placement there.

That errant growth needs trimming now.
It's better soon than late.
Wounds will heal strong when loved,
And fester more when they are shoved.

When prayer is used to guide the growth
The outcome is assured.
Failure does not cross the path
Of those who've nurtured without wrath.

Nurturing the rising generation is not unlike nurturing a bonsai plant. Nurturing a bonsai plant involves patient cutting and trimming over time at just the right time, in just the right places. It's aim is to create a beautiful, artful, miniaturized version of a plant that will fit in a "tray garden." The aim of nurturing the rising generation is to create a beautiful person whose soul is pure and inclined towards righteousness. The timely nips and cuts required in both are lovingly and knowingly administered.

NURTURING FAMILIES

In some homes o'er the world, whether grand or quite small
Are found families who know how to act.
For they know that their kindness can help all feel tall
Ever saying what they must, but with tact.

In all homes such as those, all who enter feel blessed.
There they know that their soul is quite safe.
Many long to reside there oft times, as a guest.
There the tongues are controlled, do not chafe.

There's a sad truth that many have felt in their lives
For in their homes harm comes from within.
For in these homes the smallest of parts, peace deprives.
It's the uncontrolled tongue — leads to sin.

Oh, how oft does the uncontrolled tongue cause great harm
Seems we hurt those we shouldn't the most.
If we want to improve, learn the tongue to disarm.
Seek the help from your own Holy Ghost.

In the quest to find peace, love and light in our homes,
Each must start with control of the tongue.
For each thought leads to words, then the hurt breaks our homes.
It can ruin all lives, old and young.

Help your own loved ones dear as the spirit directs.
First you master your tongue, show you care.
Then you show them your love, heart to heart, it connects.
You can do it with patience and prayer.

Part III

Poems to Give You Strength

DOCTRINES OF THE HEART

In a church, in a church, in a Christ-centered church,
The parents are taught; their teaching is reinforced.
In a church, in a church, in a Christ-centered church,
Believers are led, never forced.

In a home, in a home, in a Gospel home,
The doctrines are taught with love.
In a home, in a home, in a Gospel home
You can feel the Spirit from above.

In a soul, in a soul, in a heaven bound soul,
All the doctrines ring true as they're learned.
In a soul, in a soul, in a heaven bound soul,
Seeds of truth will seldom be spurned.

In a heart, in a heart, in a Christ-like heart,
There's a need to reach out and share.
In a heart, in a heart, in a Christ-like heart,
His strength will ever be there.

THE POWER OF LOVE

Lyrics by: Jacque Leonard

Music by: Jacque Leonard
Arranged by: Jacque Leonard

2. How long could we keep up this pattern of Love?
Behavior could fit us all, just like a glove.
Just practice each day with your thoughts then our tongue.
How good would this be for the old and the young?
Chorus

3. Don't all of us long for a world so sublime?
Wouldn't homes full of kindness be more than just prime?
Just think of the impact on families all 'round,
If parenthood meant that such love would abound.
Chorus

4. We all can do better, be kinder, praise more.
This pattern takes thought and hard work at our core.
It's worth it for all with a wish for more peace.
It could be that home peace would slowly increase.
Chorus

LETTING GO

It feels so good to be in control,
Being in charge of my life.
I know just what needs to be done,
By me and everyone else.

If only *they* would do and think as I direct,
The world would be right,
And they would see — surely they would see — if only. . . .

Well, it *would* feel good to be in control
If only they would let me.
Oh, why they won't listen?
It's okay to be in control — isn't it?

Perhaps — just perhaps — my life would be better
If I just was in control of me.
In control of me — how would that be
Just me in control of me?

I'm such a complicated thing.
Can I truly accomplish even this and feel good?
Control — Control what?
To what or whose standard?
Is control to me the same as control to you and you and you?

Is my source of good and guidance the same as yours?
Wait — A thought.
Who's really in control here?
Could it be that He, who made us all,
Has a plan for me?
If so, how can that plan reach its highest and noblest end,
If I strive to wrest control from Him
And retain it unto myself?

What? What's that you say?
I can be in control of letting go?
Yes, I can let go of *them* — my control over *them*,
And I can let go of control over all
That won't help me fulfill His plan.

This I will do.
I'll control that part of me
That would lead me away and teach me not to pray.
I'll control that part of me that will teach me to think and search for His will.
This I can do!
It feels so good to be in control — of me.

Wisdom

Have you ever felt "I can't afford, it's not fair?"
Does it seem that those words hurt too much?
Just, perhaps, it would help if you knew of their source.
Truth could help, so you'd tell self, "Beware!"

Please recall that there's one who desires you to fail.
His great plan? To remove your free will.
You were given the power to turn from his wiles
And avoid being robbed, forced to quail.

To avoid being trapped by his vile, luring ways,
You must stay in control of your purse.
Pay your tithing, spend less than you make every time;
Learn to save, lead your heirs through the maze.

Choose this path. You'll have freedom from fear of debt's trap.
Lives of servitude won't be your lot.
Pay your debts; join the growing crusade to be free.
Then reach out and help friends 'void the strap.

CALLED TO TEACH

From time to time we may be called
to reach beyond ourselves
To teach and touch another soul
beyond our comfort walls.
It may be hard to do this task,
may seem beyond our strength,
But if we heed the call to serve,
His love will know no bounds.

Each soul on Earth is dear to Him,
more precious far than gems
For Him to reach into each life,
he needs our willing trust.
So if you're called upon to teach,
to reach beyond your norm,
Say yes, and lean on Him to show
you how and what to teach.

SELF-MASTERY

When we have overcome the world,
We'll sit upon a throne,
As Christ did also overcome
And now sits on His throne.

Convictions of the Gospel truths,
Lead man to master self.
Because he knows that God doth live,
He made us like Himself.

We strive to learn, to understand
How great we really are.
This gives us strength to do what's right,
And reach for Heaven's star.

This helps us choose in every case
The path we're going to tread,
Before temptation comes our way
And tries to turn our head.

From time to time we all do fail;
And Satan plays his role.
He whispers that there is no hope
He'd love to claim our soul.

Just reach up to the Heavenly throne
And ask for Father's aid,
Then take the path the Gospel shows,
That plan, before you laid.

Incline your heart toward righteousness.
It's worth the effort made,
For you are God's beloved child.
You have the strength; Christ paid.

Reserved Just for You

There's a warm special feeling reserved just for you;
If you want to receive it, here's what you must do.
You must listen to hear, 'gain, the still little voice
That whispers to you that you now have a choice.

That still little voice can be felt in your heart.
It leads you to know He has giv'n you a part.
(Because you are His feet and His mouth and His hands
And your neighbor is needing to know where you stand)

When you heed that small voice and go forth and you share,
Then your neighbor reveals how you answered her prayer.
There's that warm special feeling reserved just for you,
Just because you did listen and knew what to do.

When you're close to the Spirit, you oft' hear that voice,
And it whispers to you; you again have a choice.
Choose to listen and make no excuse 'bout your life.
All those things will work out and there won't be much strife.

Then you will be amazed at the joy you will feel.
(To all others who watch you, it won't seem quite real.)
So cash in on that feeling reserved just for you;
You just listen and do what He wants you to do.

One Heart, One Mind

Lyrics by: Jacque Leonard

Music by: Jacque Leonard
Arranged by: Jacque Leonard

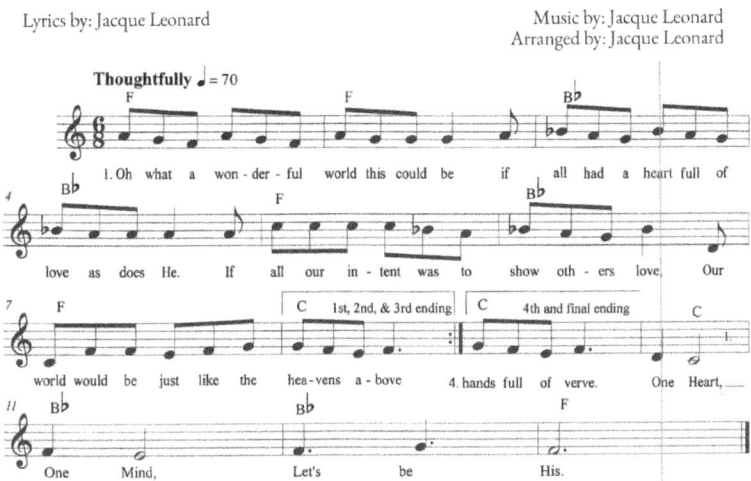

2. What if our mind had but one guiding thought,
To find ways to serve just as Jesus has taught?
We all can find ways to be gentle and kind,
To push unkind thoughts from the front of our mind.

3. Scriptures relate a few times in the past,
When people lived like this but it didn't last.
Although the whole world isn't ripe for this peace,
We can make a choice our contention to cease.

4. Choose every day to show love in your home,
Despite paths the others have chosen to roam.
Keep front in your mind the desire to serve,
Then you'll be a tool in His hands, full of verve.

One Heart, One Mind, Let's Be His!

Integrity Matters

Life was young and I had much,
Though my battered old car said less.
I worked at a lodge in a mountain town;
'Twas a place of much renown.

Summer was o'er and I headed home,
Just me and my battered old car,
And in the back were three white towels
With the crest of the mountain lodge.

When I got home, I was greeted with cheer
'Til my dad saw the three white towels.
My heart felt dark when I heard the words,
"I expected more of you."

The very next week I coaxed my car
Back o'er the tortuous route.
No words were said, but I felt clean,
And knew my life was changed.

Never again could I be led to take,
And not give proper due.
It's deep in my soul that the right way to live
Is to honor the best that I know.

How can we help such integrity grow,
If it's not planted deep in the heart?
This is the time for all men to prepare
To meet God, who sent us here.

Eternal Families

If you have a father who loves you dear,
And he leads you and guides you toward heavenly sphere,
Then you have a glimpse of a heavenly intent
Of a Father who'll hold you when this life is spent.

If you are a girl with just such a dad,
You are blessed, for no better can e'er be had.
Just search for the man who can match that same mold,
And give the children the blessings such righteousness holds.

If you are a boy with just such a dad,
You've a duty to be that for your own lad.
Remember the model and hold to it tight.
It's a pattern that leads down a path that is right.

What if you're not blessed with just such a dad?
Does that mean that contentment just can't be had?
Not so! You've a choice of the way you will live.
Just become as He guides and helps you to give.

When families show love that is deep and pure,
Then their place in the heavens becomes quite sure.
For families are meant to be linked through all time.
When there's love, there is nothing can be so sublime.

Eternal the family is meant to be.
There's a pattern in Heaven for you and for me.
Just love in obedience and teach children how.
Ask for guidance, then follow. Make it your vow.

INFLUENCE

Think of those who've influenced you,
Shown you much that you should do.
Surely many you recall
Who helped you stand so very tall.

Some were teachers from your past.
Friends and neighbors were'n the cast.
Influenced you for good or ill.
We all can find them, if we will.

Think who sees you as a gem.
Know that you do influence them.
Know they watch both word and deed.
Your influence is not a weed.

'T'sup to you how you'll be seen.
No one can escape — come clean.
Do and speak with conscious thought.
And then your life won't be for naught.

Jacque Leonard was born in Coeur d'Alene, Idaho, in 1945 and knew from a young age that she wanted to teach. After earning her Bachelor's degree from Whitworth University in Spokane, Washington, she built a long and meaningful career in education from 1967 to 2001, teaching students from preschool to high school and later training adults as a corporate educator. Jacque is also a Distinguished Toastmaster, an accomplished cellist and composer, and a lifelong lover of language who has written more than 140 poems since college.

Alongside her professional life, Jacque and her husband opened their home to 17 children during the 1980s and 1990s—some for just a few months, others for several years. These included children of friends in crisis, youth in need of a safe place, two Native American girls whose families sought alternatives to boarding school, and four international exchange students. Now living in Northern Idaho with her husband and daughter, Jacque continues to be active in her faith and finds joy in her nearby grandchildren, creative pursuits, and the enduring power of sacred verse.

Rachel Rounsville Christensen (b. 1996) is a representational realist artist specializing in figurative painting and impressionist landscapes. After receiving a Bachelors of Art from Brigham Young University in 2019, she pursued training in representational drawing and painting by apprenticing under master artists Patricia McMahon Rice, Susan Lyon, and Casey Childs. She's been recognized by the Portrait Society of America and Southwest Art Magazine's 21 Under 31: Young Artists to Collect Now as an up-and-coming artist and her work has been included in exhibitions across the US. As she's traveled throughout the world and lived in different communities, Rachel's art has been inspired by the incredible people she's encountered and the way they shape the natural world around them. She currently resides in San Clemente, California with her young family.